THE
WEATHER-BEATEN
SCARECROW

James Finnegan

Doire Press

First published in 2022

Doire Press
Aille, Inverin
Co. Galway
www.doirepress.com

Layout: Lisa Frank
Cover design: Tríona Walsh
Cover art: Mantas Poderys

Printed by Clódóirí CL
Casla, Co. na Gaillimhe

ISBN 978-1-907682-91-9

We gratefully acknowledge the support and assistance of The Arts Council / An Chomhairle Ealaíon.

CONTENTS

For Livinia

Seven-Thirty This Morning

a distinctive *courleee* sound
    then into view
        a single curlew
flying with purpose
    toward early morning pastel greys
        the curlew lit from underneath
by scattered dawn light
    a high-pressure sun fingering liquid gold

yesterday driving home from Bloody Foreland
a northwestern hill of slanted pink and russet brown
    life moving on with Michael gone
I leave my body   the ghost of me
continuing the drive home
    a lone plaintive cry
    & single flight
                enough to lift me

Lingering Wells

twice   caught by surprise
   down to climb the Reeks with John and Martin
I head for a coffee in Killarney

sit at a table by a child's high chair
pull it in rather than push it away
   in a flash   there's a presence

and an absence which move and hold me
   chest-tight squeeze of my rib-caged heart
a forgotten dialectic making its mark

the quiver beneath my skin
   we tried and tried and did not succeed
a humanity no less qualified

   that was May   this is July in Lahinch
   having a meal with my in-laws
I hear a girl say *Mammy*

I cannot see her   hidden to our left
   my eyes well again   again I'm held
this time   it's about you not having a daughter

I Don't Believe in Angels

I push against
the ash branches
of morning
and evening sky
folding back
in my stretch for
the good dark
in things
the felt unseen
whispering
through the atria
releasing
some suited angel
in hobnailed boots
crumbling earth
grounding
grinding pretend-time
I am almost certain
I am not
out of my mind

The Poplar Leaves are Unafraid

Michael would have been sixty-five today
next Thursday I see sixty-seven
   if I am granted a long lifespan
I will write for another generation

some of my notes from an inside back cover
   more prayer   more silence
go for a run   shave the beard   small things
   to help me keep alive

once again   out for a walk   pre-sunrise
a fire-coal red behind eastern grey brushstrokes
the moon in the west changing from yellow
to platinum gold   to white

a gibbous paper moon cloud
faded on the south-eastern side
   early on   the sky a faint lilac
a thin grey veil that has purpled

the padding of our springer's walk on tarmac
the crunch of my boots on gravel
the quivering of two birch trees
   fifty metres apart

shaking like poplars but not much to say
apart from *I am moving in the wind*
& maybe   *I am not afraid*
which I guess is something

a book of poems by William Carlos Williams
arrived yesterday   wary of an imagist bind
he stated his intention to write
whatever whenever & as he damn pleases

the sky mostly clear now
 where there is colour   a light grey blur
clouds' edges change from fire-glow red to nimbus orange
 as the sun rises   & *Hello*s everything

Between the Silences

I trust myself to the shocked
leaves in mid-September
    to the darkness which chokes the evening light

I trust myself to the quiet
on Inch Lake's water
a month before the whoopers return

I trust myself to the optimistic
& hope-filled hop of our springer
    a female guide who shows me the way

I trust myself to an un-named tree
in the corner of our garden
in whose limbs I rest after the last long cut

I trust myself to Kinnegar Strand
& its conclaved quiet
where an unleashed spaniel is freedom's hound

I trust myself   to this lived life
        this undiminished brief
            between the silences

Wacchen-Clocca

the clock's lips are thin
    and grim
as quarter after nine
      and eerily
    your six o'clock kiss
runs the length of your face
    and where is the eye
of *Under the Eye*
    is your soul business
      to keep alert
and where is your bell
      as you can't yawn
        I take it
    you never tire
are you conscious of
    every tick every tock
        or are you immersed
        in this room
    watching me watching you
      in the pure presence
          of eternity

Out Feeding Horses

so it begins   Easter Monday
April the 24th 1916
park keeper James Kearney
feeds the ducks in St Stephen's Green

the Irish Citizen Army
take over the Green
    lodge in the College of Surgeons

on a different side of the Park
British forces
busy themselves into the Shelbourne Hotel

hostilities are lifted daily
to allow keeper Kearney
to feed the waterfowl

when asked by de Valera why
he isn't fighting   Grand-dad says
someone has to feed the horses

the rebels take over
Boland's Bakery   the horses are let go
along with cats and dogs from
the animal welfare building next door

de Valera and Company C
feed the animals
    when the foodstuffs run out
    they are released
onto the streets of Dublin

Mrs McDermott sees her old dog
wandering by the Liffey
    for the first time
he doesn't come when called

mallards zig-zag and upend their way
through the six-day rising
    only a *little perturbed* by the gunfire
      when all the firing stops
there are still horses on Sackville Street

Daring-Do Diary

summer of *All You Need Is Love*
a packet of *Charms* and ten cigarettes
on the way to the beach in Spiddal
alongside a tide-flow of young
after language lessons in Colaiste Connachta
    fourteen going on fifteen
in the presence of girls
                  but not in their company
steal a *James Bond Dossier* from a local shop
fantasize about smoking Peter Stuyvesant
Bond's *car* and *drink* of no interest to me
    my coat goes missing at a *Ceili* one evening
take great pleasure in expressing much annoyance in Irish
       I think I find it eventually
    cycle down a lane with no brakes
straight onto a main road
in front of a car crawling at 5 miles an hour
fall in front of it   but am fine   and lucky I guess
    second-last night   one end of a belt around my neck
other end around the neck of a large bottle of *Cidona*
    guitar hanging across my back
I climb down a downpipe beside my bedroom window
for a party outside a nearby graveyard
    a crowd of us are caught
    my guitar confiscated
collect it from the principal's house next morning
    mid-day he addresses the whole school
    Ba cheart go mbeidh náire oraibh go léir
so pleased I understand the meaning of *náire*
    even if the Tipperary girl doesn't like me
                that summer I had a great time

Dry Bones

there's no word coming to me
nothing distinctive on the rise

I feel I have nothing left to say
as if the inchoate is locked in bone

a frozen marrow wilderness
waiting for life to happenstance

yet there's confidence
water will again flow from stone

the yellowing horse-chestnut tree
the leafless ash with red berries

tar-spotted sycamore leaves
montbretia October-ing through

brilliant fuchsia fuelled and felled
ivy stealing light and water

holly admiring its own green shine
crisp curled copper colours rustling the road

      looking at the out there
      brings me back every time

Water & Wood

surrounded by multiple barbs
the still-living fencing post says
    being isn't everything
the spinning cockerel weathers the storm
sometimes facing east mostly southwest
    yesterday it crowed
that surely it's more than an embodied I
even the ants are aware of a secret
    long hidden from me
as they scuttle toward an upturned ice-cream cone on the sidewalk
always upping the ante of being more than the singular
    even too the shy giraffe sticks its neck out
to claim there is something more than itself
but it's the fast-flowing streams   the rivulets
    & the oceans
in their sweet intermolecular binding
that know a wholeness way beyond the one
    each bare branch in winter knows too
there are a billion others like it
and that the surrounding air
    though part of it is more than it
by the old theatre the rustling leaf
blown along the ground
    goes as far as whispering
there's a good beyond being

Ghost Dance

I ghost dance back to that red-brick house
to the time when we called girls moths
    and played on the street
from where we could see the Wellington
    the girls kick an empty tin
    and hop between chalked boxes
and sometimes we join in

I approach the pond where we once fed ducks
    below the hill of lazing daisies
        the birds anchor me now
    one coot carrying nesting material
to the other building on the pond
    a seagull snatching
paper from the swimming coot's bill

a lone cormorant swims from one end
as if it were the only bird in the long pond
    mallards mingle in their routine way
        the coot continues to build
seagulls stand by in nuisance mode
    moons and moons ago we walked here
        but the present insists on itself

a swan grips the sneaker of a young father
who playfully offers its white rim as food
    tufted ducks synchronize dives
    and surface in individual style
a moorhen with red and yellow bill
    and hidden lime legs
        shimmers the water into a painting

Madra Rua

Natural History Museum   London   seventies
top of food chain   Ecology Book
red waistcoat   cigar   glass of rosé

today   russet brush   your back to the road
other part of the predator prey relation
explosive call   followed by   a goodbye whine

whiskers on your legs   help you find your way
you lay there yesterday   near the same place
but closer to the edge now

no differential equations
take account of the main predator
of you and yours   by a bloody mile

I saw you once   tiptoe   happily red
on the long front lawn at Manresa   by the sea
at home   with purpose   unafraid of me

The Wonderful Blue

a teal-coloured bin from Challans Vendee
with a typical French-turn aesthetic
collects papyrus   make that   paper
tossed by the hand of the poet
crumpled and squashed with varying pressures
first there is *manifold*   folded at *man*
next   *suicide* with *ici* to the fore
which hurts more deeply when it's near
    her husband having died first   six months before
third   *metapoetic* with *tap* in bold
turn on   turn off   in search of lost ground
then   a caesura   the welcome while of waiting
    fifth   *circadian rhythm*
    where all that is seen is *circa*
sixth   *elegy* with an exposed *leg*
remembering the distinctive walk of the dead
finally   *heaven-sent*   with that *heave*
            of effort involved in living a life

Thirteen Things I Get From Charles Wright

one
it's okay to sit on a chair
in the back garden and stare
at whatever unfolds before me

two
the shadow of death is not black
but blue like shadow on snow
in *The Magpie* by Monet

three
landscape   language   and the idea of God
without the weight of a description of being
have a part to play in opening a door
                              to a good beyond being

four
there's a glorious rhythm to thirteen syllables
which is something plucky and not at all unlucky

five
a seven-syllable line is often followed
by six or five or eight or ten syllables
or seven but rarely four
or there could be thirteen or fifteen

six
that upper white clouds can shatter
makes it possible to imagine
hearing and seeing that shattering from afar

seven
there's a breathing beat in getting older
while not letting old age in
someone has suggested staying active and interested

eight
my hair can grow for one hundred years
and make me speak like a prophet

nine
the rain washes each description of itself away
quicker than a moving mouse refresh tap

ten
the spectacle of the particular isn't always storied
but more often storeyed like palimpsest and pentimento

eleven
deer and caribou and weeds and grasses
move in the air and can bob and whelp

twelve
each morning I can sit where I always sit
and it is never the exact same
a long patience has made it so

thirteen
there are thirteen other things and thirteen more
the final one here listens to an underground hum
an ever-freshening world at work in the naming of things

The Humming Word

after Wisława Szymborska and Mark Strand

there is something burning
below the sternum
just to the right of the heart
    a thirst
I guess a hunger too
but mostly thirst
a yearning for a doorway
out of darkness

I varnish the iroko gate and doors
spray the white dash of the house
can't hear the hum
of anything passing by
someone empties the septic tank
jet-sprays the percolation pipes
the gurgling sound is a gurgling sound
and no more
then silence
in the garden

I don't interrupt
I have no words
to carve with my tongue
no hum   nothing to shape

nor am I a body
enwrapping a song
only the hound of the ordinary
inchoate searching for an understate
dead oak leaves on the ground in July

A Palimpsest-Pentimento Parchment

after Richard Kearney

it was claimed by some
there are word layers on the left
and layered etchings on the right
both made with similar crafting
the upper left layer declaring
the word mesmerised by a mirror
on its right a fading blindfolded face
milk and oat bran wash through to the next layer
to the left *the word refers to the thing*
beside that the face of a woman with an eye-patch
third layer *the word is the thing*
to its right two-faced Janus
final layer the grey-white space of no word
next to that looking at what's before her
the wide eyes of Helene Schjerfbeck at fifty-three

The Winds Dance

at night I lie on my left side
facing north   I guess that means
I'm delivered feet first each morning
to the east   as are you
as the earth continues its turn and tilt
suppose for a moment we become
what's in the direction of our gaze
I face the Arctic you the Antarctic
I am a sea of ice surrounded by land
you a frozen continent
surrounded by saltwater
some say we complement each other
another has suggested there be spaces
     in our togetherness
twenty thousand kilometres
we have the whole earth between us

Breaking Free

the dusty brown stallion
stands by splintered wood
    a van turns
the horse charges down the road
    then charges up again

our neighbours walk
through the broken fence
grab his bridle
    lead Adam home
saying they should never
      have got rid of Eve

Adam on a Good Day

I go for a run on the longest day
    Adam ignores me when I call
seems to be sulking since Eve left
or   more correctly   was taken away
    is it possible to talk horse-sense to a horse
I run on for five kilometres
meet a grey cat who rises
with her two front paws
purrs   and pushes her head
into the palm of my hand
    one kilometre later   a golden Labrador
walks towards me and stops to be stroked
and continues on its way
    for the record
Adam has run to me before
and sticks his head over the gate
to receive longer greener grass
which I feed him   and maybe stroke his face
so   a horse   a dog   and a cat
show me affection (apart from Adam today)
        and I them
    more than enough   to lift me

    on this longest day
I also read two books of poems by the same writer
    I get the clever cutting-edge talent
    however
I'm not held
like *Falling Awake*
holds me
    or like a lovely grey cat holds me
or a golden Labrador   or Adam on a good day
    or even Adam on a day when he ignores me

Shadows and Ghosts

in the early 1900s
a tribe somewhere in Central America holds
someone without a shadow is a ghost

feeds into one of Carl Jung's archetypes
    Hermann Hesse views
sadness as the shadow of a cloud

it's said Ms Liu was murdered by Mr Ma
sold in North China for 35,000 yuan
as a *minghun* ghost bride for some dead bachelor

Dennis O'Driscoll in *Dear Life*
casts a steely stark eye on the dark
where there's no false saving grace

Philip Larkin with an eye of sorrowing
reads real gloom in the room of things
blows cold and cold   and filtered light

Amartya Sen and Tripping With Daisy

Amartya Sen draws us to capability and freedom
    if I have a car outside the door it's only then
that I truly have the freedom to use it or not
I may decide to walk the dog and not drive
      having a car gives me extra freedom
        to accomplish what I value
going from here to a more distant there
    not on a whim though that too
but when my freedom of movement needs a stretch
    and also for other reasons
      I guess I could choose a bicycle
but it rains a lot here   not for the full day and not every day
    why not a bicycle and a car
which I have but we walk our springer spaniel three times a day
so I either walk or drive but don't cycle much these days
    and her eyes look directly into our eyes
and lower the freezing point of our hearts by several notches
    and raise the level of love hormone in our bloodstreams

Slender Thread 1974-2004

polyethylene terephthalate
stretched   twisted   octagonal cut
driven away in long green lorries at night

24/7 before 24/7 became a cliché
Courtaulds then Unifi   scrambled to Asia
faulted the local economy

molecular chains drew the workers in
metal chains on gates keep the workers out
all seven hundred   another hundred before that

Keith McClean and Eddie McCarron
seek jobs elsewhere   as does Michael Crampsie
the bright grey polyester plant eventually flattened

A Tiny Spider

I have just finished reading
Heart Transplant by Miroslav Holub
a tiny spider takes in the next Czech poem slantways
from the last line toward the first

with right middle-finger and thumb I flick it
into its future and out of sight
until I see it making for the edge
across the circular Costa tabletop

switching from killer mode
to Saint Francis mode
I lay two croissant crumbs on the table
which it bypasses

I lift a burgundy leather glasses case
out of its way
onward toward the edge
and over the side

where it lowers itself
on an invisible thread
only to climb back up immediately
having judged the floor

to be too far away I guess
or maybe the sight of my face
under the table
was sufficient

it disappears again
until I catch view of it
on the back of my left hand
nothing sinister there

I lay it on a ledge
near the floor
but it is still attached by a thread
and moves with my hand as I pull away

I lay it down again
and off it goes into a future space
safe from at least one
fickle finger-flicking human

Burying Our Cat

her last evening   Elsie came to greet me
she rolled on her side   let my hand stroke her
    four sods on orange plastic   soil on blue
    a small deep grave ready for the next day

sedative   then anaesthetic OD
administered by the visiting vet
so it came   that she was lain
in a back-garden corner within sight

I'd bought two copies of *The Irish Times*
one copy for me   the other for her

The Year of Water

first I thought it was the sound of a drill
but through a hole in the ceiling
water thundered onto the kitchen floor

my mother-in-law's house   & in my own mother's house
an overflow tank flooded the bathroom floors
got that sorted with a telescope ladder to the attic

third   the percolation system in our garden
    the air vents filling with water
sorted that with a new drain to the left far corner

then there's the river-flow in Raymond Carver's poems
more broad-shouldered than holding back on what one means to say
& there's another poet's *Nobody*   at sea   with no resting place

last there's a poetry editor who favours profusion
living with someone who favours precision
one can't help wondering what their love-making is like

Soul

that which is silent
often in enforced absence
need not be silenced

Szymborska   Simic
are not afraid to mention
it   why should I

Joyce said to Nora
no one stands as near to it
as you   that's something

it may be absent
a good deal of one's life
but turn up now and then

mostly exhausted
from wide wanderings over
fire air earth water

baffling
impossible to express
even in stillness

present in seeing
itself never fully seen
leaf-blown from a tree

shy   non-invasive
landing like air on soft grass
in a whispering

Old Giraffe

there's a hunter with a strange brain
and razor-blade mind
who shot an old giraffe in Africa
and posed with painted blood through dark hair
whilst surrounded by the majestic kill

there are other hunters who do the same
this hunter   in-your-face   Facebooked it
with gun-hunger and deadly aim to tease

and claimed   the giraffe   a herbivore
can be a dangerous animal
and also claimed to feel a connection with   her kill

Nunavut

you might ask how a researcher with *Climate Rage*
landed on an ice floe in Baffin Bay
      in July 2021
but here I am now   drifting towards Bylot Island
there's a research station there
   I was examining a ringed seal air hole
in the ice when this chunk broke off
   more-or-less oval shaped
100 metres long   60 metres wide
I have warm clothing and some food
     it's summer
   there's a polar bear swimming by
who has just decided to climb aboard
   a large male with some blood on his snout
     much to my relief he stays his end of the floe
I do not move   and wait   and wait
   and after two hours he re-enters the water
and swims away
in the direction of Greenland
   Francis Jack   an Inuit friend from Pond Inlet
rescues me an hour later
     I'm glad there was no need to add to the red

At a Stretch

Dr John Coghlan   PhD John
and not GP John   taught me how
to stretch an elastic band against
the fresh-shaven skin above my upper lip
and feel the cooling   the lowering in temperature
    as strands straighten and become more ordered
    a decrease in entropy   the opposite of
                the usual tendency to disintegrate

    which makes me think of chaos in Cairo
and wonder if the traffic there came into line
    could that by chance help generate
a decrease in global warming
    though Bangkok   New York   and Beijing
            might also have to hum along

Alphabetically Yours

after Iggy McGovern

from afterbirth to aftermath
from beetroot to bloodroot
from confusion to profusion
from eye-and-ear to pioneer

from fission to fusion
from hippo to hip-hop
from income to outcome
from jobless to homeless

from Ku Klux to Cuckoo
from lantern to lanyard
from Mandela to umbrella
from overseas to under siege
from Pantheon to penthouse

from quarterdeck to quarterback
from rain check to pay-check
from sickle and plough to tickle and howl
from unskilled to deskilled

from wasteland to waistband
from xylem to asylum
from yes men to Yemen
from zoom in to zoomed out

Arkle
1957-1970

Mary Baker sells her loved three-year-old
bay gelding who delights in galloping
    small working group   nobody hurries him

    not a bad move in his body
ears point to the sky   a high head carriage
a way of looking out at the world

    in the stands hearts pound   and   silence
broken by gasps at each galloping leap
    you know I think we might have something there

    excited chat on factory floors
and building sites   and public houses
    that's our horse   *that's the Irish horse*   *up yours*

    the racing British like him too
Ireland is absolutely bloody good
at something   Arkle   out on his own

final race on Boxing Day sixty-six
runs two miles with a broken pedal bone
                flinches just before the finish

Never the Lost Face

is there really a window to the soul
   is there really a soul
   certainly there is a face
which can in part reveal
     a lifeworld
   a living dust of personhood

when the scythe's shadow passes
   many chase heartless deadlines
as they paint the lost face with light
   but David Douglas Duncan
   a marine war veteran and
  Picasso's photographer friend
      urges
   nunca   nunca   nunca

House on Olive Street

faded yellow wood   peeling roof
white clotted walls   floorboards post-sneeze
a fox-shaped trivet as a door knocker—
two bushy tails like hands with thumbs-up
    Julia Child's home in forty-eight
    and fifty-six to fifty-nine
Olive Street   the only street in Georgetown
        named after a food

    a renovation specification
states that there must be enough space
in the kitchen to slaughter   cook
    and cure a 250-pound pig

houses have bones   houses have souls
        though Julia's gone
    it seems the kitchen houses her soul

Early Morning Rise

my sandals crunch the gravel
as I turn the garage corner
catch the scent
of the oil tank
the back of the house
dead oak leaves on the grass
dying oak leaves on the tree

cold November air
stings my face
slaps the back of my calves
below my long black coat

Elsie yammers   spins   purrs
croaks a meow
busies the side of her cheek
against the back of my hand
    hunkered down
my knees touching wood
I squeeze my hand
through the rustling plastic bag
extract a handful of cereal

lay it on
a happy etching
on the base of the bowl
the purr driven munch begins

the bright band of light
in the eastern sky
above orange tinged grey
waits for us to roll its way

I check the cat's house
fill the water bowl
go back to bed
but on my way
decide to shower
and head downtown
for a cappuccino
by a large window
in a new coffee place
made mostly of glass

Asymmetric Understanding

our friend who has just had a six
hour operation tells us
that for every hour   a month
of recovery is needed
which means he'll be fine
     by December
unsure what to say next   I say
our new springer spaniel is three months old
     and for each of those months
we can leave it for an hour on its own

Operating Room

I think it was Francis McNutt's *Healing*
     before or after he left the priesthood
which nudged my mind from an either/or cell
through an open door to a both/and world
     or at least its possibility
as sometimes the choice *is* between two things
     as in *wanted dead or alive*
but let's assume none are being hunted

I have seen Charles Simic offer a choice
     at the end of a work
say between someone talking or singing
     or in another work   the choice between
lingering over drinks or heading home
     and long before that
John Fowles in *The French Lieutenant's Woman*
provides two different endings   that was

nineteen sixty-nine when many wondered
would The Beatles break up or not
     and long memory
keeps putting them back together again
two gone   not half the group they used to be
and the shadow cast comes from more than one thing
          thank you Mary Oliver
     in the other direction   there's *only* one thing

which can back one into a corner
     a modern-day Isaiah has given
     his anti-monist take on
'The Pursuit of the Ideal'
while Paul Simon proposes fifty ways
     to leave a lover
and finally   the song and dance man's call
it's either this or that or neither of these at all

Inglenook

there is a small space beside a fireplace
where I sit alone and dream of fire
    blue flame hotter than yellow
    sky colour cooler than the sun

moons and moons and moons ago
I walk Land's End with Michael and claim
    Penzance is full of crooks and nannies
    and wonder what would Winston think

        and yes   we laugh
        and all the world hears
                your big laugh still

An Alphabet of Starlings

there are twenty-six birds on the wire
    an alphabet of starlings
watching me through French doors
as I read Nan Shepherd's *The Living Mountain*
    I look up again and they are gone

there's a lone crow on the ground
now the crow   a chaffinch   and a collared dove
then the same crow and a wood pigeon
I open the door and clap my hands
    they fly away
in flits a brave coal tit scout
to peck on hanging birdseed
followed by flits and chatter
of landing and leaving chaffinches

a passing tractor
chases all away
apart from a solitary wagtail
more sure of its ground than I

Nan Shepherd says bird watching
has to do with moments
of their lives that have crossed
with moments of ours

which   in whistles and silences
and chatter and flits
and waiting and absences
and presences   and more waiting
    probably means much more than
two sets of beings watching each other

Feast Day of Saint John the Baptist

a lot of people know the joke
    about the difference
between a hedgehog and a Mercedes
filled with five guys wearing sunglasses
    the hedgehog has the pricks on the outside
which is fine   and well we may laugh
    but today on the way to Lough Barra
I came across a hedgehog who'd made it
    most of the way across the road
a soft spiky hemispherical hump
        with a pool of blood by her head

Spent November Light

sadness visits me like a bird on wing
    all I can do is let it fly its way
        spent November light downs me every time

crows gather under three birdfeeds
    the broken hare loses its springing frame
        a young chick chokes in a steel cylinder

four deer on Farscallop watch us walk in the chill
    no saving grace in the northern hemisphere
        winter is winter and wills autumn gone

the month mourns the lost hour of evening light
    thirty nights bereaved and bereft
        as slow grief bleeds the lone wolf's howl

and if that hour were given back
    and the red hare restored to life
        I would willingly give up holding it

in my hands and the feel of its warm blood
    and its falling and rising ribcage
        and my closeness to its big brown eyes

Striding Edge With Daisy at Ten Months

up from Glenfidding
on the way to the top of Helvellyn
a steep craggy climb
     Striding Edge
like the back of a Stegosaurus
Daisy our springer & I venture
   umbilical-ed by a leash
of trust
   & a measure of fear
the kind that concentrates
      eye   & breath
  times it is pretty hairy
sometimes holding her
   both of us   ledged
       looking down at a death drop
   other times   backtracking to weave around
     more often   doing it slant
  to lessen slope & fear of fall
    all the way to
a lower path leading to another higher back bone
    the relief
         of winging it
            to the top of Helvellyn

A Lone Crow Up High

yesterday   up high   I saw a buzzard stalk a lone crow
the first time I've seen this happen near our home
I stopped the car   got out   clapped my hands
as I watched the two glide on

    nearby a small murder was gathering
    as the lone crow's tension tightened

within a minute   the flickering cluster of crows
    at least twenty   multiple peck the perplexed
raptor   who moved sideways
    and sideways again   and then   away

Exhausting Joy

the female springer sees
the childless couple
   and thinks
I will not be
   your child

I will show you
my face of sadness
   accompany you
      as far
       as the dark

A Posteriori

fainting goats faint for a reason
not a reason they themselves
have thought about
they fall over
then quickly pick
themselves up again
it is not a case
of I can't go on
& then I'll go on
but rather
I fall & rise again
to munch sweet meadow brush
& isn't that a good
enough reason for a fall
in the first place

The Simple Arithmetic of Our Lives

after Charles Wright

no particular reason
these things were in the wind
by the broken bench below Skiddaw
up from the village of Applethwaite

if anything adds up it vanishes
    as speedily as the present
I guess one could say
there's nothing much here

each here with its instantiated breath
    the tufted duckling
swallowed whole by a hungry heron
says there are now three and not four

a hard lesson in subtraction for its mother
    that magnetic pull no longer heard
if it's not a heron it's a rat
yet we still multiply

knowing that inbuilt minus
    sooner or later
will make our absence felt
we're all undivided in that

Lime Kiln Cottage Autumn 2021

by Lough Derg a red squirrel
with fox-coloured torso
and dark bushy tail
crosses a road near Portroe
farther north a pine marten
crosses near Ballingarry
Lime Kiln Cottage a clear night sky
without artificial light
    over Terryglass old cemetery
a high wispy French sky
a white cloud fold pattern against blue
clearer than a water colour
    a while before migrant geese return
Canada geese feed among the cylinders of hay
a young springer flushes a pheasant for the first time

Blue Shadow

where is the light in the darkness
is it on the far side of the river
                          or is it this side

someone has written about the good dark
        changing the nature of darkness
like coloured shadows on snow in Monet's *The Magpie*

there's a dark door in Schjerfbeck's *The Door*
        a line of white upper left side
but it's the warm glow down low which draws

another has said the virtue of hope is existential
        & what difference does that make
is there something more than feeling at work

in drawing oneself up out of the well of drowning

The Living Room

yesterday morning   out walking the dog
a crow lands briefly on top of a gate
bringing to mind a painting by Monet
The Magpie   perched on a gate in a wattle fence
     sunlight on snow creating blue shadows

now in a framed print on the wall
to the near left of where you sat
     richer than the lone sorrow of a single magpie
     & opposite you   a large clock
so you'd know the time when the carers called

when June came late you'd call her July
     above the clock   a large photoprint
     a sheep on a hill looking at the photographer
& eyeing the eye of a fox below
     the image titled *watching me watching ewe*

     to your front left   a teak elephant
I carted all the way from Thailand
     in the summer of 1994
a solid steady presence by the television
sometimes carrying magazines on its back

when you were ninety-one you needed help
     sense of humour vibrant as ever
after I first called you asked *when is the greyhound coming back*
     you could tell Livinia it was snowing
by the shadow of the falling on the far wall of the room

The Face of Vincent

a face   not yours   comes through
the café door in Dungarvan
and reminds me of you
fifty years ago
when my father let us go
to Dockery's for clothes
and you   Vincent   served us
shoes shirts trousers
belts and jumpers
with grace
and the face of a humble angel
and how is Brendan
and Michael and Bartley and Mary
and where is Brendan living now

Dockery's closed down
I remember seeing you
once at church   unusually unshaven
    and then you were gone
only last September Bartley told us how
    at a loss of words for you Vincent
you who wrote what we purchased in a book

Otto Nove Dieci

someone has said
there is always more order
in what we narrate
than what we live through

there is a lone table & a lone chair
in one of the local Costa cafés
I pull in a second chair for a coffee
      a social absence before me

as I drive home I drift into thinking
I am on a train   it stops at a station
   I get off   no one else there
only the warm air   the platform   & me
         & the leaving train

I think of the packed station in Old Delhi
    passengers fan their faces
a power-cut at five in the morning
      total darkness
the train guard tells me to stay where I am
another waiting before a silent stranger

once I drove from Interlaken to Cuneo
    from a town of old age
to a town of laughter & talk & the loved young
      we camped in the Italian Riviera
a group of children stuck their heads into our tent
one of them taught me how to count to ten in Italian

we never saw her again   I guess life is like that

Wishing Well

my mother got me *The Courage to Be*
by Paul Tillich   after my father died
   it's the only book my mother bought me
I read enough of it to understand
something about being and nonbeing

over thirty years later Charles Wright mentions
that emptiness happens & that it often occurs
    along with a sense of nonbeing
& in an interview   Hannah Arendt claims
   that it is natural to have enemies

   so   reflecting on suffering
     that acute kind
where my particularity is hated
   by one who ignores me
   with no hope of dialogue

   the sharp metallic cut
of the absence of love
   I dig deep   to love my enemy
     & in my nonbeing & emptiness
              wish them well

The Man Who Brought My Father Up

from the time my father was eleven
Mortimer Kane   primary school principal
married to Bibby Kane née Murray
    worked in the same school
    Inverin   barony of Sailearna
lived in a house of the same name
known as Uncle Murt   who cycled all the way to Cork
    for a hop step and jump All-Ireland championship
which he won   gentle as a Kerry breeze
in soft rain and who used words like *gasúr* and *forage*
who knew Padraig Pearse from further west
    later I'd call to see them in Renmore Road
    pork chop   apple sauce   and a half crown
Murt   tall man in a suit   quiet river-flowing presence
I once talked to him about girls to which he replied
    Sure you can forage over the summer gasúr
        member of the governing body UCG
days when primary school teachers were small gods
but to be clear   Mortimer Kane was a genuine force for good
    another time I asked him what local difference
the 1916 Rising made   to which he responded
    with shining light in his eyes
                        the price of butter went up

A Short History of the Week

although much more than light
I make light from the lightest

there's a moon ribbon in my hair
as I mount a mustang mare

I did not choose Tyr's way with words
nor a war with Mars

the ravens of thought and memory
leave my shoulders each day
reporting back each evening

I am a thunder cloud
waiting for a lightning strike

I am earth's twin and Odin's first
sulphuric acid in my breath

I am wide rings of ice and rock and dust
scarecrows at rest in the fields

The Butterfly and the Raven
after Franz Kafka's The Hunter Gracchus

for thirteen days we climb in Parc National de la Vanoise

I do not track a chamois
nor attempt to follow one home
as luck would have it
moving on up from Col de Chavière
August the twelfth 2011 I encounter a single chamois
the only one seen by us in our time there
I do not ask if it has seen the hunter Gracchus
or the hunter's fall into a ravine
or a raven bleeding to death
where the hunter fell
or a butterfly fluttering from the dark
it's eleven years since I've seen
that chamois at ten thousand feet
the butterfly is gone I expect
though some say it still lives
on a bier on a boat out at sea

lying there wave and tide with no plans and no self-blame

Colour Me Beautiful

it's early November
four whoopers honk overhead
the swan at front taking a quick glance
back to check they're still all together
after a 13-hour flight from Iceland
heading to Inch Levels
where they'll stay until April

the springer & I come across
a small pond with an arched bridge
four tiny moorhens with yellow and red bills
& hidden lime legs trying to hide
the remainder of themselves
a male & female mallard nearby
appearing huge in the water

by the fields I come to realise
the rams are not wearing braces
but ram marking harnesses
with slabs of bright-coloured crayon
to keep score of their encounters
    on the rare occasion   all colour
& no lamb   outing an infertile ram

Sparkling Dark

wherever the river flows
wherever the water goes
    life is teeming
so the daily missal confides

before I woke up yesterday
isotropic was in my pre-fall
I look it up later
discover I know its meaning

the same physical properties
whatever direction you travel
    that that which/who is known as unknown
may be isotropic is of no help whatsoever

I guess it is sufficient not knowing
    last night I told someone
about a Jesuit weekend
I once attended in the late eighties

it was Halloween
and I happened to get the ring
in the barmbrack
    and then hear women sing

enough sparkle for me to discern
    along with Billy and Mary Rose
calling with a present for my new home
               as if to say *don't go*

Being Human

being human has given me
this still moving space my body occupies
the time of my life I have on earth
a sense of balance and some nerve
a way of walking that's recognizable
  I'd know it anywhere

being human has given me
uttered words which slide in the ears
    and shape their way into my brain
    so this is how I speak today
these are the pictures in my mind
Kansas   Kansas   and then some Oz

bird-whistle and full- and filling-leaf in May
the grey cat pushing its head into my palm
the lick of a busy collie during its working day
the sparkling water both sides of a bridge
new-born Friesian calves and lowland lambs
        apart and at peace in the same field

the pass-over of four curlews
on their way to feeding ground
I cannot fly   but your wings lift me
    being human has given me
solid ground
    often the only thing I trust

I've been given an accompaniment
of others on separate islands of existence
my feet apart   dust scattering
on desert sands   as micro-worries are blown away
    where's the bond of connection between things
a lot say there's no Love   but me   I'm not so sure

Beatitude of Littleness

the steel cylinder of bird food
      pendulum swings
the scent of coffee wafts
       in the cold January air
the young springer makes easy work
   of a plastic chew
the chill on top of Errigal
   slices at least twice
we slide on our bottoms
     into a valley of snow
   first five-kilometre run
with the spaniel today
   I run   she walks fast
I become less
     as the world becomes more

Beatitude of Witness

let the stone of emptiness be your bed
the stone of sadness let it roll far from your door
let the stone of despair crumble and disappear
feel your heart chambers beat their bloody beat
keep your balance as you displace the air
    feel the charge-flow from earth
push through the soles of your feet
    do not be disheartened
or diminished by a fleeting lifespan
let the stone of hope anchor you
    it is said the existential
lies deeper than the psychological
let the stone of courage lift you
      do not be afraid of a happy life

The Weather-Beaten Scarecrow Leaves the Field

I've something to say how will I say it
where does this something come from
the words are mine   but from where the meaning
    that line from a Jesuit priest at Manresa
in my wondering about imagining what the Lord says to me
    usually I hide that I'm a believer   I don't know why
maybe like holding back in contemporary tone
often present in poetry art and drama
and really good Australian movies
    just after missing the turn in this sonnet
definitely not holding back there
someone has said there's always more order
in what we narrate than what we live through
when Elsie died I realized she had one life and not nine

when Elsie died I realized she had one life and not nine
that arose in a resurrection poem I wrote for her
and cats hold back   was Elsie holding back on eight lives
someone else has suggested we go from Kansas to Oz
    start with a blade of grass then cut
to some philosophical thought
that it works well to anchor in a concrete image
another has said it's either one or the other
    or neither of the two
unsurprisingly there are two Kansas Cities
the main one in Missouri – KCMO
the other later founded in Kansas state out of envy
    its tie unmatched to its shirt
a weather-beaten scarecrow leaves the field

a weather-beaten scarecrow leaves the field
a turn or two it takes to calm its tattered mind
I imagine this scarecrow will not return
Professor Pam Lomax once said to me
I never ever contradict myself
unless I change my mind
but that is not the turn of mind I have in mind
more like the road in David Hockney's *Garrowby Hill*
or *The road to York through Sledmere*
or a road somewhat less than a Pauline Damascus
a bend a turn a twist something that keeps one awake
and lights a fire in the next beat and breath
    this or that or neither this nor that but
something richer fuller than has happened until now

something richer fuller than has happened until now
    you're now entering the geriatric phase
    this is where I overtake you
    it's a pity your talents are scattered to the wind
from my beloved Livinia ten years younger than I
along with the humour the number of syllables charm me
the great Charles Wright has taught me to love the longer line
a plucky rhythm to unlucky thirteen
varying line length   utilizing a breathing beat
calming caesura giving a breather between breaths
    sculpted sound shaping the code of silence
    meaning trumping structure every time
maybe it's time to gift the scarecrow another tie
the brilliant white cockerel always facing into the wind

the brilliant white cockerel always facing into the wind
often spinning in the eye of the storm
I go figure the I-figure and write from there
maybe seated on a chair in a back garden
or sitting on a bus in the city
or walking along a country road
pitying all the lambs who don't see
themselves as future food
and all done with a holding back
not the open-heart sleeve of Raymond Carver
and when I weep it's my eyes that tear not me
     or I may be a talking tree
not needing permission from anyone for that
but what of those who wish to drown the I

but what of those who wish to drown the I
I know one is not meant to explicate
     here no explaining but an opinion
I see language trapped in a post-structuralist cavern
where the word is not the thing nor refers to the thing
but looks solely to the word itself forgetting the human
so it's no surprise if some wish to dissolve the I
deliberate disorder of the disorder we live through
linked to dissolving the I is dissolving the narrative
it seems some have stepped off a postmodern ledge
     into a narcissistic wilderness of negative mesh
I'm weary of clever-clever writers with no I
no story   no history   no human who
and what of the expressive mode of treatment of the poetic

and what of the expressive mode of treatment of the poetic
    that which takes us into a wonder-realm beyond words
layered consciousness   layered paintings   layered writings
    not mere *palimpsest* and *pentimento*
but deep structure   the rooted doings and beings of things
first we see   then the words   but seeing comes first
please take us to those layers below and beyond words Lord
sometimes the way in is through a cup of coffee
more often   in through the chime of the mimetic
    the pleasing sounds that wave our ear-drums
and then on into the chest and rib-cage
    and maybe the head after that
the weather-beaten scarecrow with neck-gaiter has a question
        I've something to say how will I say it

An Ordinary Morning

the spaniel and I walk as far as the cottage gate
painted silver   a short grey wall on either side
    woollen hat on my head
the sound and cold of an east wind in my ears
the soft grounding of the dog's paws on tarmac
    swinging tail and purposeful walk
my own polyurethane soles beating an iambic rhythm of sorts
swollen stream down to the right low-thundering along
    long after the equinoctial rains of September
a mid-October dryness to the road
twisted maple and oak leaves rustle by
    resting low by a recently cut conifer hedge
five young calves shelter from the wind
Adam the horse whom I fed grass to yesterday out of sight
    lack of clouds gifting early morning brightness
hands in padded jacket pockets
leash round my left wrist steering the dog and me back home

ACKNOWLEDGEMENTS

Thanks are due to the editors of the following publications in which some of these poems, or versions of them, have previously appeared: *New Hibernia Review, The Irish Times, Chasing Shadows* (Lapwing, 2022), *Local Wonders* (Dedalus Press, 2021), *The Stony Thursday Book* (2020), *Cyphers, Southword, The Cormorant, Skylight 47, The Honest Ulsterman, Boyne Berries* and *Drawn to the Light.*

Thomas McCarthy has had a huge influence on my work since June, 2017 in Listowel and continues to be a great support and inspiration. Kevin Higgins has helped me tweak a number of the poems. Deirdre Hines is a poet-friend and confidante with whom I have many discussions about poetry and writing and who has kindly taken on the task of reviewing this collection.

I am deeply grateful to Thomas McCarthy, Deirdre Hines, and Audrey Molloy for writing the back-cover blurbs.

A special thanks to artist Mantas Poderys for the image on the front and back cover of *The Weather-Beaten Scarecrow*; I think it is an extraordinary piece of work. I guess it's okay to say that I am the scarecrow and also not the scarecrow and that springer spaniel Daisy is Daisy at all times.

I appreciate what John Walsh, Lisa Frank, and Tríona Walsh of Doire Press have done and are doing to get this collection of poems on the move — thank you so much.

JAMES FINNEGAN, Dublin born, was the second-prize winner in the 2022 Gregory O'Donoghue International Poetry Competition and was shortlisted in the 2021 Bridport Poetry Prize and in the 2018 Hennessy Literary Awards for Emerging Poetry. A sonnet, 'The Weather-Beaten Scarecrow', was published in *The Irish Times* in August, 2021. James, who taught in St Eunan's College for thirty-three years, holds a doctor of philosophy in living educational theory from the University of Bath, and is now retired and has grown into a deeper commitment to reading and writing poetry since November, 2014.

James and his wife Livinia, along with their four-year-old springer spaniel Daisy, live a few kilometres outside Letterkenny in Co Donegal.